I NEED YOU

I NEED YOU

REALLY, I DO!

Bill Caldwell

Bill Caldwell can be reached at
caldy3@verizon.net. He would be happy to
hear from you.

To order additional copies of this book, contact:
Xlibris Corporation
1-888-795-4274
www.Xlibris.com
Orders@Xlibris.com
39800

To all the "you's" in my life and to those yet to come—

And to John Anderson, my friend, who helped me get the stacks of 3x5s onto these pages.

CONTENTS

PREFACE

Maybe you are wondering why I chose the title I NEED YOU. It is the "you's" in my life who have let me get thoughts down on paper that otherwise would have remained locked away.

Many are dear and close friends. Others are casual acquaintances. Still others are the multitude of people I've interacted with—or simply observed living their lives—over the years.

What follows are random thoughts, and they are random, written on 3x5 cards starting in 1978—mostly in public places—and still happening almost 30 years later. You will not find any startling wisdom—just thoughts that swirled between my ears at one time or another, in one place or another, ending up on these cards.

For me it has been a great recreation. I traveled a lot on business and had the habit of taking along a stack and re-reading them. They were sort of like talking to an old and trusted friend to whom I can express stuff without asking too much of his patience in a face-to-face.

If there are some words here that strike a familiar note that support your own inner thoughts then I hope it is good for you to know you have company.

A SMILE

A smile.

How beautiful if given.

How sad if withheld.

CRYING

What's wrong with crying?

It can cleanse not only the eye

but also the soul.

TRUE LOVE

How can one give so much to another

yet believe he has only received?

It is called true love.

LONELINESS

Loneliness is ever present in human existence, yet the remedies abound in a thousand ways.

We go through life feeling this need for human contact but don't see that we live in the center of the answer.

Loneliness is the result of internalizing one's life.

The way to avoid it is to reach outward in thought and deed.

The void then will be gone and the cup filled.

SEPTEMBER 20, 1978   SOMEWHERE

PRESSURE IS . . .

Self-induced

from too much

from not enough

from distorting what is—

and, the rarest of causes—

real and true pressure.

JULY 10, 1980   DRAKE HOTEL—CHICAGO

SHOES

Given the choice

thrown in the ring of life

I choose my shoes for the fit.

What a lucky man am I.

THE VOICE WITHIN

The voice that is within does say
"Oh, follow me—I know the way

to live your life as it must be
will give you vision so you'll see

that any other path you take
will only cause your heart to break."

No secret then of what to do.
Unto thyself thou must be true.

AWESOME

The power of positive thinking is awesome.

As is the opposite.

Positive thinking should be so simple.

Why is it so elusive?

PEACE OF MIND

Peace of mind—what a great thing to have in the space between our ears!

Its value outweighs things material by giving the possessor an inner well-being beyond all else.

FACING THE WIND

Stand to the wind.

From there comes

The freshness

The challenge

The opportunity

The breath of life.

FRIENDS

They come in all shapes and sizes.

Wide is the variance and depth.

They are precious jewels to be cherished and cared for.

How lucky is he who has friends in his life.

OCTOBER 8, 1989   ARMANDO'S RESTAURANT, CHICAGO

THE MIND

We can leave the mind to its own devices; just a living organ functioning the way it must.

Or we can use it, challenge it, reach into it toward its unlimited depth.

Yes, sometimes the delving brings questions—even turmoil.

But it is worth making every effort to open that mental door to whatever might be there.

THE STEPS OF LIFE

_____ Infinity

_____ Old Age

_____ Maturity

_____ Adulthood

_____ Youth

_____ Pubescence

_____ Adolescence

_____ Childhood

_____ Infancy

_____ Birth

SPECIAL BEAUTY

Observing the energy and innocence of little children is one of the most beautiful beholdings in life.

What a shame we have to grow up.

LIFE PASSES

Beauty surrounds us yet remains unseen.

Lost in the preoccupation of living.

Thus passes by the rising and the setting of the sun.

And of life.

Too hurried are we.

PUTTING OUT

Putting out is often the key ingredient in a new relationship.

It is also the key if the relationship is to last.

Mostly physical at first—more multifaceted as it matures.

But putting out (giving in to) a lasting relationship will be the measure of its success.

HAVE YOU EVER NOTICED?

Have you ever noticed the way the trees, flowers and grasses bend in their growth toward the sun?

And usually the side that reaches out to the nurturing of that great source of energy is where the beauty of its blossoms burst forth.

Not unlike the human form who possesses the power to see, care and do for others.

As you reach out seeking the privilege of giving, so shall the beauty in you flourish and grow.

INHIBITIONS

Inhibitions—what a waste of time!

Try "going for it" without them.

You will surely have a lot more fun.

And by the way, so will the people who know you.

MARCH 19, 1986   REPUBLIC, MEMPHIS TO NYC

SMELL THE FLOWERS

Ah, we must make time in life to smell the flowers.

Usually, our worldly pursuits preoccupy us so that we never see, much less smell, the beautiful blossoms that pass by us each day.

The flowers that I speak of sometimes come in strange forms. Perhaps in a fleeting smile from one who holds a door open for an instant so that we may pass.

These individual blossoms pass by us in abundance each day.

Trouble is, we seem to see the weeds much more readily.

ON YOUR MARK! GET SET!—GO!!

High can be as high as we make it.

Of all obstacles that may impede the climb, those that are self-imposed are most likely the ones that can keep us from knowing the mountain top. There is a capacity within each of us to make the impossible possible.

Get excited—very excited! Life holds possibilities for you that will be limited only by your ability to dream, to believe, to set your goal and to go about making it happen.

Wow! What fullness is there for the believer in life.

What do you have to lose? Give it a try.

On your mark! Get set!—Go!!

I LOVE

Oh yes, I do love.

I love life.

I love you.

If I cannot love you

I cannot love myself.

If I cannot love myself

then I cannot love anyone.

YUP!

Yup, it can happen if you believe it will.

Without believing, life is quite barren.

Hang in there!

Hope and try.

It can be.

It will be!

CAREFUL

It is not a good idea to form opinions about people in bars.

They are most likely responding to physical and/or emotional needs of the moment.

Thus the observer will not see the wholeness and worth that may well be there.

I NEED YOU

I need you, I fear to say.

Ah, what weakness and waste are the inhibitions in us.

DECEMBER 22, 1995   GRAND HYATT, NY

GO FOR IT

Why not go for it?

What else is there to do?

Lie down? Roll over?

Not me.

To the wind will I stand.

TURN PROBLEMS INTO OPPORTUNITIES

The first step in changing problems into opportunities is a change in attitude toward the goings-on in our lives.

We must sort out and prioritize so that things become manageable.

Then, with a firm belief—"All things are possible"—go forward with resolve.

Self-doubt is a human characteristic that can bury us in self-created defeat.

If you feel overwhelmed at the moment,

Take that first step.

Change your attitude.

SAILING

No two sailboats run life's race the same. Even if seemingly identical they differ, however subtle it may be.

Add the skipper and the very great differences in performance grow from narrow margin to ocean's breadth.

The boat responds to the wind, wave and current but most of all to the holder of the sheet and tiller.

How he plots and points his course will lead him to his port of call.

How sail you?

FOG

Fog rolls in from ocean to land and thus to touch man.

To some she is a haven to slow life's journey, for only a fool ventures forth in sightless striving.

To others, she is but a small inconvenience.

To still others, she is a great frustration as the fog slows the course set.

And for a very few, there is a special beauty in that rolling mist of nature.

She comes to remove from sight all that is there so she can then lift her blanket for us to see anew what truly does surround us in all its God-given magnificence.

How rolls the fog for you?

TRY (TO OPEN UP)

Patience is to know the way
How to pass through life each day.

Treading softly as we go
Seeking out the goal we know

Leads to where we want to be
So that inner joy we see.

Often oh so hard to bear
Having no one there to share.

If our needs we hold within
Life itself cannot begin.

Courage, yes—to open up
So life then can fill the cup.

Risk of hurt may well be there.
Take the chance lest life be bare.

TO STRIVE

Tread the water or swim on through?
Float through life—is that what you'll do?

Against the current will you stand?
Stroke out with courage as you can?

For the effort is worth the try.
To strive brings peace so you can lie

Safe in the knowledge you have done
The best you could. The battle's won.

TOUCH

What a beautiful form of expression a touch can be, if given—not taken.

For, as in anything that is of real worth, it must come from a giving posture.

NEW SHOES

At first fitting, there is doubt.

The mere fact of newness is enough to make us return to that which is familiar.

But then what will we ever know of the cobbler who fashions the shoe as it truly should be?

MAY 31, 1979   AMERICAN, KANSAS CITY TO NY

OPEN UP!

Open up to the beauty around you of God, nature and man.

Have the courage, take the risk to see, to touch and to know.

Do not let life pass you by through your lack of strength to—

Open up!

CAN DO

Oh, the power of a "can do" attitude!

There are few forces more potent.

Unleashed against all adversities—be they fiscal, physical, objective or subjective—

"Can do" shall prevail.

SHELF-BOUGHT SHOES

There was this lady walking with two canes.
One shoe had a sole about 8 inches thick.

The bus driver waited as she rushed to get aboard.

With a happy smile she exclaimed, "Wow, am I lucky. You waited for me. Thanks so much!"

She is crippled in body but surely not in mind.

Quite a lesson here for those of us who buy our shoes off the shelf.

WHY ISN'T EVERYTHING PERFECT?

Why isn't everything perfect?

Because it isn't.

If it were—

How sad.

ADVICE

Advice so freely given, so hard to follow.

Why can we counsel others yet not ourselves?

To see their predicament yet be inwardly blind.

Does the nearness of the tree make the forest impossible to see?

How see we outside with vision so clear—yet know not the self that is so near?

DIVERSITY

Thank goodness for diversity.

Without it the world might tip over!

ISOLATION

What is it that finds us isolated one from another?

Inhibitions? Circumstances? And the saddest of all reasons: because it doesn't make any difference to us.

We who are human are not fulfilled alone by the animal within us.

Our human quality is measured by our need for one another and our willingness to give so that what can be—what should be—is.

TIME PASSES

Three minutes of time has just passed us by.

The speed it travels—the blink of an eye.

How then is it spent? What price do we pay?

God's gift to the living

squandered away.

MAY 31, 1983   HILTON HOTEL, COLUMBUS, MS

DEALING WITH INEQUITIES

There are ghosts—of the past—and the present.

What has been—was.

What is—can be changed.

It is for us to make right what is wrong.

Start with today—yesterday is gone.

Today's demands (met honestly—and with action) will require the best of
the humanness within us.

THE SOURCE OF LIGHT

Diamonds sparkle best from the inside out.

Like people whose inner glow is so much more than the outward show.

TO FRIENDS

Friends. What a beautiful word!

People blessed with friends have in their possession one of life's greatest gifts.

To have a friend—a real friend—is a special beauty often passing us by never to be known.

Ah! Here's to friends!

ULTRAVIOLET LIGHT

The magic of ultraviolet light transforms that which is into that which
dreams are made of.

This light, in a way, is physically false.

Yet it takes the ordinary and creates beauty—

which is there all the time

if we will but behold it.

THE SOUND OF SILENCE

Silence is in the unheard word.
The voice that reaches—yet, not heard.

A special sound both loud and clear
for one who listens thus *does* hear.

In life we hasten to and fro
knowing not just where we'll go.

But this it need not really be
if only we would stop to see

that there is sound and sight in man
for us to hear and see we can.

But such a goal if we will know
can only come from what we sow

The giving out is what is meant.
A gift to us that God has sent.

FATHER AND SON

Father and son—head resting on shoulder—

smile on face—trust, a belonging.

Sneaker to shoe—love showing through.

What beauty is there!

JANUARY 12, 1995   BAREFOOT BOY, PUERTO RICO

THE FOUR S'S

Sea, surf, sand and sun—

how they can bring calm and comfort to one's soul!

THE HAPPY MAN

How much the happy man warms the lives of those he touches.

A touch that may be but a passing smile—or the mere sight of him and the warmth he passes on.

Who is he? How did he get this way? Is it all an accident? Is it because he is just simple?

Or is it because he works hard to be the way he is? And, if he does—why?

No, he is not simple. It is no accident.

He has learned God's secret that life's gift is in giving.

And the sight of a happy man is truly a gift to those who behold it.

For it says happiness does exist and is possible.

ON RELATIONSHIPS

How rich are they in a relationship so deep it lets them be angry with one another.

So much more than not caring at all.

FEBRUARY 27, 1983   PS SAN FRANCISCO

THE DRUM

Dance to the beat of the drum.

Who is to say what is the beat?

Can the beat be known only by him who hears it and thus responds?

There are so many ready to strike the drumhead expecting all to march to its tune.

Go only to what *you* hear.

TRUTH

Truth—how very elusive!

It hides behind all those things

we think we are

we wish we were

or

feel we ought to be.

JANUARY 10, 1986   (FINISHED JUNE 4, 1987)

A THOUGHT

Sometimes we dwell too much on our negative relationships with people or on unfortunate situations in which we find ourselves.

Perhaps the lesson here is that we need to accept what is. If the situation is negative, recognize this as part of life and go on from there.

Life is for living. And, depending on the state in which we allow our mind to dwell, living can be a joy or life can be left wanting.

SPONGE OUT

Oh, that we might sponge out of life all that is there, for the world is full of goodness and beauty.

But often we are like a new sponge that has never known the touch of life's moisture.

And when we first meet its fluid, we do not absorb what is given us.

Yet life's flow is patient. It rests waiting until accepted and then slowly sinks within us—giving life and meaning.

This porous being softens from rigid, arid immobility and comes alive.

Now ever sensitive to the merest drop of living dew that touches its surface.

And thus is born one who can soak up life's beauty as it rains forth from all that is there.

FRIENDSHIP (AGAIN)

Friendship is a very special gift.

It is especially beautiful when we are given the opportunity to return it.

And when we do so—not at our convenience—then the privilege to do this takes on the meaning of life.

THE HARP—THE LADY IN PINK

Is it the sound?
The image of the angel's instrument?
The setting?

Or is the harp a thing of special peace, sound and sight?

Its music strokes and caresses, soothes and gives rest to ear, mind and body.
How special is its ability to do so. Perhaps it truly is of the angels.

What of the lady in pink? She plays in this commercial place, yet as I look
at her there is an expression of the harp upon her face.

Even as she glances at her watch, it is not as other players of music do.
There is a quiet, restful return to the producing of this special sound.

Perhaps it is in part how the harp lies upon her shoulder. There is a
closeness, an intimacy not shared with its sister instruments.

The lady in pink has a very special beauty. The lady in pink, who plays
upon the harp.

CHOSEN COURSE

State of mind in my control.

How it will be mine to call.

To the wind I choose to stand

for there is no better way.

DECEMBER 23, 1981   T. J.'S

WALK SOFTLY

Walk softly passing by.

Step with care lest you tread on those who stand upon or cross your path
for they are special beings in your life.

A chance is given for you to know of thoughts and hopes that flow within them.

From such a source there is a richness and knowledge of those who have
passed by.

Treat it with care and caring.

THE WANDERER

He passes by us all the time.

Far more often than not—unseen, unknown—as we busy ourselves on our journey through life.

Yet, to know the wanderer is the essence of who we are and why.

But most of us are too preoccupied by what is just the tip of the iceberg of life.

APRIL 7, 1981   T.J.'S

KINDNESS

Be kind to yourself, for in doing so you will know how to be kind to others.

And as this giving moves from you to another, then you will know life's fulfillment.

And why you are here.

PATIENCE AND PERSISTENCE

Patience and persistence—never forget them.

For if those things important in your life do not seem to fall in place—

Be patient.

Be persistent.

ON CLOSE RELATIONSHIPS

Who's right? Who's wrong?

Maybe both. Maybe neither.

No two relationships are the same.

In a close and caring relationship these differences can be very pronounced from time to time.

Perhaps the answer is to recognize this is as it is and go on from there.

PUSSYCATS AND DOGGIES

Pussycat, pussycat, I don't like you (as much) as I like doggies.

I think this is because you only come to me when it suits your needs and never mine.

I like doggies far more. For it seems doggies are (almost) always ready to give their love.

SEPTEMBER 1981   UNCLE CHARLIE'S

THE FLOWER

See the blossom flower and then mature

Where it remains in the beauty of its fullness and knowing.

HOW WE PERCEIVE

Fresh-blown snow comes sprinkling down
from above upon the ground.

There to rest in beauty so
thus it is that we can know

there before us we will see
most true gifts are really free.

So tarry, friend, be aware
great are the things waiting there.

Reach for others, that's the key.
What you give will make it be.

Nothing special here is said.
Simply stated, cast thy bread.

CIRCLES

There is this thing about a circle

It always returns from whence it came.

Is this like life?

To end where it began?

If so, why is the journey so unkown?

WHERE FROM HERE?

What has gone before—has gone before.

We, you and I, really cannot change that.

But what we do have is from this moment on.

It is ours to do with what we will.

We can dwell on what has been—what might have been—what should have been—but it is past—gone—done.

What is left is the rest of our lives. It is we who have control over how that will be. If we look to the negatives—so shall we reap. But, if we take this day—this moment—as an opportunity to see and be part of the beauty that is there for us—

then will we be given—through giving—

a happy and fulfilled life.

LOOK UP!

Shoulders back—sit that way.

For such a physical stance is good for others to see.

It speaks to life and gives hope rather than the slouch of the downtrodden.

So, look up! Besides, it's good for you! ☺

MARCH 17, 1989   COMPANY

"OH WELL"

Ya know, how really appropriate "Oh well" is about many happenings in our lives.

We, individually and collectively, have such a tendency to overcomplicate things

when the perfect perspective is just—"Oh well."

THE SUBWAY MUSICIAN

What is more important to the subway musician,

the clap of the hand or the dollar in the hat?

I think both.

But if he has the stuff of material well-being

then the clap of the hand is much more important.

THIS TOO SHALL PASS

This is to be read when depression has set in and you are unable to shake it.

The message is as simple as it is true: This too shall pass.

My state of mind is now good—very good. I am on no particular high—just a comfortable feeling of well-being.

But I remember well how hard it is to be in a depressed state—and most of all how difficult to overcome it.

There are many things we can—and should—do to fight this negative posture. But I am not sure there might not be a somewhat immovable time frame that needs to pass before this low period can be cast off.

If this be the case—that time must pass—then perhaps our most comforting support can come from the realization that:

This too shall pass.

COPING WITH WORRY

One of the most powerful tools for coping with worry is to make a concentrated effort to focus only on those things you can control.

Then put them in perspective (as best you can) and deal with each within your capacity to do so.

If they are overwhelming, then seek help and support from others.

This done, you have done—

your best to cope.

I NEED YOU

It is the "you's" in my life who have let me get thoughts out and on paper that otherwise would have remained locked away. Many are dear and close friends. Others are people who may have crossed my path ever so briefly.

To all, I say thank you for helping me get out what is within.

I need you—and I care.

FLYING THOUGHTS

Thoughts that flow in flights through sky

often come, I wonder why

seated on a plane at rest

from the day now decompressed.

Inner thoughts what it's about.

Writing it removes self-doubt.

What is "it" the question be?

"It" is what in life I see.

EACH DAY

Why do we go through each day without an appreciation for the very fact that each day is *given* to us?

It is ours to do with what we will. Some days are filled with challenges—problems—or are they really opportunities?

If we start each day aware that it is a gift to us—then will it be filled with what we put forth to make it the best we can.

MAY 28, 1979   ROLF'S

YOU HAVE PASSED BY

You have passed by and I know not what is within.

You have passed by and I have missed the chance to understand.

You have passed by—and I care.

THE GIFT OF LIFE

How do I accept it?

How do I live it?

Do I merely use it?

Or worse yet, do I badly abuse it?

Do I remember life is God's gift to man?

Do I remember to pass it on?

Have I learned He intends His light to shine through me?

What wattage do I give for others to see?

OF CORE HONESTY

To live life as one truly sees it is both rare and an act of inner strength.

Often it demands a cost few are willing to pay.

If it is honest and the price is paid, the inner peace can be of special quality.

But—there are traps requiring constant vigilance if true core honesty is to be achieved.

What is *your* core? Is it what you say and what you feel—or merely think you feel?

Has it been masked by certain elements of your life so that what seems to be you is not truly you?

Are you unwilling, afraid or unable to truly acknowledge the you of you?

Of the more serious traps facing the core seeker—

Are you taken up more with the mechanics of acting life out rather than living it?

The degree to which this trap is avoided is in direct proportion to true inner peace.

INNER PEACE

If I could pass on the peace that is in me as I write these words, how happy I would be.

And, darn it—how happy I would be if I could manage to just hold on to it myself!

For, as unphysical as it is, inner peace is not an easy state to maintain.

It is thus I say I'd like to pass this moment on—

But I'm afraid it is so fragile and fleeting that each of us must blow our own bubble and let its reflected beauty shine for us.

However brief it may be.

OCTOBER 23, 1981   ACADEMY, LOS ANGELES

STEADY FRIEND

My pen is my companion.

Not always available but most of the time.

My pen is no pushover. Often it is very demanding and critical.

But usually honest.

APRIL 13, 1981   COMPANY

SWEEPS
(THIS TITLE WAS WRITTEN IN 1981.
IT IS NOW DECEMBER 3, 2005)

Now, as I reflect some 25 years later, I know why I wrote this title.

The reason is the amazing effect that sweeps of mood have on our lives.

They can run the gamut from great elation to deep depression—

yet nothing physical has changed.

Wow! The mysteries of the mind!

OPPORTUNITIES

Gosh, think about the unending opportunities given to us each day to reach out.

They abound far beyond our capacity to give.

The giving may be nothing more than a smile to a friend or to a stranger.

Or the holding of a door a millisecond for the one who follows.

Maybe unnoticed—but sensed.

HOW TO OVERCOME SHYNESS

It's not easy, but possible.

If being shy is keeping you from reaching toward the fullness that life holds, then it is worth your courageous effort to overcome it.

First, try to visualize the good things that might happen were it not for your fear.

Are they not worth going for?

Whatever your reasons for not being able to expose yourself, they do not need to keep you from changing.

If you will try, you will find that your negative anticipation is almost way less than expected, and, far more likely, you will experience a positive result.

But nothing will change if you do not take action.

The greatest defense for one who is shy is to procrastinate.
There are no limits to the number of reasons one can find to not act.

Start wherever you have to. There is no need to challenge the lion in your first effort.

But, above all, start and start now.

Believe and act.

You have little to lose and so much to gain.

A FRIEND IN DESPAIR

If there is a friend in despair, give comfort. For he who despairs desperately needs this human compassion.

Let him know you understand.

Reassure him that things will change, and those negative elements that now overwhelm him will melt in the warmth of perspective and the passing of time.

A SIMPLE ANSWER

The need within every human being carries each of us through life searching for fulfillment, when all the time we are surrounded by the answer.

Simply stated, it is what is within that is given out.

From this source will come the meaning of life.

SNAP JUDGMENT

Snap judgment can be a very big mistake!

Oh sure, there may be some truth in first impressions.

But, as good as they may be,

The risk of being wrong says

"Don't do it."

Don't discount a person on the basis of an unfavorable first impression.

For you may miss an experience that might well be a thing of beauty.

REALIZE

Realize what a privilege it is just to wake up in the morning.

What lies before you depends on what you will make it be.

Yes, there will be those days when despite your best efforts, things just don't come together.

But remember, life is a privilege.

Soak it up.

LIFE'S JOURNEY

If you are confused as to who you are or who you wish you were, take heart.

Such a state of mind is very isolating but you are not alone.

You are like most people at various times in life. Uncertainty is not an easy state but a necessary one if you are to reach close to the person who is you.

It takes courage, strength and a willingness to explore those most tender and vulnerable parts of your inner self.

This exposure can be a difficult experience, but it also can be a richly rewarding one.

If you will open this door into yourself, there can be found a path that is yours to follow.

And in so doing you will come nearer to the meaning of your life.

If you accomplish this—you have journeyed well.

TAIN'T EASY!

No, sure tain't easy.

A relationship—almost any close and meaningful one—just plain is not easy.

If it is between two people living and loving together, it asks more than most people can or are willing to give.

Aside from our instinctive selfishness (self-preservation) there are all the genuine differences in personality, culture, emotion, intellect, sexuality—and more—much more.

No wonder the ups and downs even in the more "perfect" bondings are there. But, as difficult as it might be, how worth the effort!

For to be without relationships—particularly a close one—is to miss the beauty that life can hold.

SOMETIME　　　　　　　　　　SOMEWHERE

JUST AN OBSERVATION

Generally speaking, people who appear threatening are often less so after conversation with them.

And sometimes those who seem frail and vulnerable are less so when known.

EGO

When does self-confidence change to self-serving ego?

How is a proper balance to be kept so that the necessary belief in one's self does not run over?

There seems to be a need within us to reaffirm our self-worth, which often ends in conflict with others.

Many times, ego is the driving force for people who achieve material success.

Yet isn't excessive ego often a lack of inward self-worth?

If this is true, then I wonder why in our order of things one who may well have an inward confidence far stronger than his egotistical associates does not fare as well in the corporate world?

It seems somewhat ironic—if not wrong—that the one who succeeds in the commercial environment may do so despite a feeling of internal inadequacy.

One wonders if such motivation often places politicians in a leadership role whose objectives are perhaps more self-serving than they should be.

NANTUCKET NIGHT

How silent is the airless night from what the usual be.

The whisp'ring wailing rushing wind and crashing of the sea.

Now carried on this silent wing a distant dog's bark heard.

And then a soft and tender voice—a night bird's chirping word.

The quietness gives a special peace that we so seldom know.

Oh magic of this special night—please linger, do not go.

NOVEMBER 27, 1978   COMPANY

HOW WE MAKE IT

How very much life is what we make it.

Each moment is ours to do with what we will.

The challenge is the opportunity.

What seems nothing can be everything.

This power is within each of us.

PERISH THE THOUGHT!

How sad it would be if the romantics were wrong.

If what flows within us human beings is no big deal.

If life and living were but of the surface.

"What is there is all that's there," says the cynic.

"Take it—enjoy it—use it—that's it.

Feelings, caring, needing, wanting—

So what? No sweat.

Take what you can get. Give what you want to.

Forget it—no big deal."

Ah, but life *is* a big deal

Says the romantic.

And so say I.

WHO IS TO SAY? HOW DO WE KNOW?

Who is to say? How do we know?

We walk through life seeing others—close by or from afar—in all sorts of forums.

And we are affected by them. We get impressions.

We wonder. We form opinions. We make judgments.

Who is to say? How do we know?

DECEMBER 16, 1987   HOLIDAY INN, CHICAGO

PERPETUAL MOTION

I wish. I want. I need.

And in return—I want to give.

It is a receiving, a giving, a receiving, a giving—

What a wonderful form of perpetual motion!

WHAT REALLY COUNTS

We are so taken up with our own daily pursuits that looking outside ourselves asks a lot of us.

But, to the degree we can look to others—to see their needs and yearnings—

And then to do what we can to make *their* lives more fulfilled.

Then will we be fulfilled.

THE END

When everything around you seems to say "This is the end, there is no more"—

Trust, believe, hang in there.

What exists today is but the prelude to tomorrow—

Which is the beginning.

ON SELF-INVESTMENT

How much will you, can you, should you invest in yourself?

Time? Money? Effort?—But most important of all—*attitude*.

The degree of commitment will be the measure of your success.

But, remember—a positive attitude above all else.

JANUARY 11,   1981 T.J.'S

STAND HERE WITH ME

Stand here with me. When I stand alone, I need you.

I am not weak, but your closeness gives me strength.

And I am glad for the need of you.

If that were not in me—I would be less.

WHAT ARE YOU WRITING?—HE ASKED

A recipe?

No—well, yes.

Not for food—

But nonetheless—a recipe.

For life.

HAVE YOU EVER CONSIDERED—?

Have you ever considered what it would be like to be dead?—

That part of what we find after we die might well be the remembrance of what has been here?

That some of heaven may be reflections of what was on earth?

How will we look back on our daily doings, one to another?

Stripped of all excuses, will our actions, thoughts and deeds—known but to us—give joy or sorrow?

In the hereafter there are no false filters of prejudice, selfishness or artificial values.

There is just the measure of acts and deeds as they are—

Bare of all but what is a bright and revealing light.

Will my acts and deeds give me peace or pain?

SELF-WORTH

Self-worth!

What a priceless possession

for without it

what can be, what might be, what should be

cannot be.

THE WAVERS

We spent the day passing through the Panama Canal from east to west.

It was interesting as we passed close by many commercial ships to see how some crew members returned our waves of greeting

while others seldom waved or not at all.

I think the generous waver is a happier man.

LET IT GO!

There are times when the thing to do is just "let it go."

Life is for living each moment—which really is all we have.

What has been—is gone. What is to be—will be.

The lesson then: Live life in the now.

MARCH 2, 1981   FLIGHT WEST RESTAURANT—KEY WEST

SEXUALITY

When you are comfortable in your own sexuality

you will be comfortable with the sexuality of others.

THE UNREACHABLE STAR

How much do we dwell on what is lacking in our life?

So often there is a longing for what seems to be missing.

I wonder, though: If all those needs were to be filled—would we then be fulfilled?

I think not. There is always a yearning for the unreachable star.

MARCH 15, 1985   LAGUNA BEACH, CA

I AM BEAUTIFUL

I am beautiful. Yes, it's true.

If I cannot believe this, how can anyone else?

If at skin level, that's nice—for it allows physical attraction to happen more easily.

But true beauty is not at skin level. It is within.

I was sorta kidding in the title but it must be true:

If I am to be able to give love (beauty), I must first be able to love myself.

HOW FOOLISH!

Sometimes there is the need to share many of our emotions, doubts, hopes and fears, for these things that flow within often need to be nourished with the food of human interrelating.

What great irony that these things remain unfed because we will not risk the opening of ourselves one to another.

How foolish!

THE SEA AND US

There is the steady roar of the surf as it breaks on the outer reef.

Closer to shore the re-formed smaller waves swirl past the inner coral.

They ebb and flow in their course that ends in a surging upon the beach.

Thus completing its journey from the mighty depths, it quietly returns from whence it came.

Like life in many ways.

The steady roar is the passing of years. The inner lagoon—how we respond to daily living.

Then to return from whence we came.

GENES

Genes—we all have them. Some good. Some bad.

That's the way it is.

Science, medicine, psychiatry—never will we fully understand how much they affect our lives.

But one thing I truly believe is that God has given each of us a spirit that can minimize the effect of any genetic makeup.

There is little that is physical or mental that cannot be overcome by the strength within each of us.

It is our challenge to draw on and use what has been given so that life is fulfilled.

JANUARY 7, 1992   NORTHWEST, CHICAGO TO NEW ORLEANS

NAKED

Be it a state of physical nakedness or a baring of one's soul—

We are left feeling vulnerable in the presence of our fellow being.

Too bad our lack of self-worth makes it so.

I AM BOTHERED

I could have—but I didn't.

I didn't make that extra effort to reach out to another.

I am bothered by that.

I guess in a way it's better to at least be bothered than not care at all.

But I hope next time I won't be bothered because the extra effort is made.

JULY 13, 1989   MY BROTHERS—CHICAGO

A QUESTION—AND STATEMENT

How sure are you of yourself?

Is it of the surface? Just a mask?

Or can you look in the mirror at who you are and say:

"This is who I am."

Then how fortunate you are!

INTERESTING (TO ME)

I realized something interesting (to me). I have been putting a lot of these 3x5 cards into my computer. As I typed I began to wonder why so many of these thoughts seemed to fall to paper in public places where other people were around.

I'd think perhaps such stuff would flow in venues where I was alone with my thoughts. I don't think it is because I am antisocial or shy. Really, quite the opposite.

Maybe it's because I wish I could express to those around me what I write but I realize that the particular moment or the place is not appropriate for such interrelating. I wish it were.

Perhaps such stuff is better left in printed form.

DON'T

A good friend just reminded me

"Don't use your own yardstick to measure another person."

Good advice!

A NEW EXPERIENCE

I went to my first poetry reading at the National Arts Club tonight. One of the readers was a Pulitzer Prize recipient and the other his teacher and mentor.

Much to my relief, I think I understood the meaning of their readings. But I am not sure I would have had I read the same words in their books.

What struck me most was the melancholy of their writings. The word imagery far exceeded anything I have, or could, put on paper.

When I think about all the stuff I have put on 3x5 cards over these past 30 years it really is "stuff" when measured by the eloquence of what I heard tonight.

Mine are of the surface—childlike perhaps in many respects. But for me some do have a profoundness. And, more important, they generally speak up to life rather than from a state of melancholy.

A GREAT LOSS

We who have been longtime friends have lost a very special person in the passing of Jack Brush.

Ever since learning of Jack's cancer, I have been affected in a way I have been unable, and still am, to put into words.

Perhaps part of it is the reality of our own mortality in losing someone we have had such a long and close bond with over these many years.

As Bake, a good friend said, "Our world is diminishing."

Jack gave me a new appreciation for how truly blessed we are with the beauty of these long and deep friendships.

So taken for granted most of the time. But a gift to be cherished.

AH—HA!

Ah—ha!

I want to spill some words to paper.
But they are not available at the moment.

This doesn't happen very often. Usually when this urge moves to the surface
it is easy to get the thoughts or feelings onto a 3x5 card.

Maybe it's good to be reminded that this mode of expressing stuff that
swirls between my ears is not always sitting there waiting for me.

SOMETIME   SOMEWHERE

THE POWER LINE AND POLES

No matter how strong the poles may be

Until they are connected by a wire

Nothing will happen.

GLUE

My mother had a great saying:

"If you're lucky enough to have the glue hold you together

all the rest is what goes on between your ears."

Wow! How true.

"HE SAID"

He said, "So maybe that's where thoughts ought to be. Internal, fleeting—left in a state of unconscious storage. Noted maybe, but surely not recorded."

I do not believe this is true. We are so hung up on our fear of exposure that we deprive ourselves and those we touch of our deep need for each other.

Why do we make such a big deal out of this need? Because we *do* need each other!

And truly, this is as it should be.

WHY?

Is it exaggerated ego or deep insecurity? Which is it that puts these inner thoughts on cocktail napkins and 3x5 cards?

I'd rather it be neither. Just a plain and simple recreation, would be a nice and comfortable explanation.

JULY 3, 1980   E.F. BARRETT & CO.

PHYSICAL PRESENCE AND WRITTEN WORDS

What is it that makes the physical passing of one's written words to another often uncomfortable?

Is it that these printed thoughts draw the reader into the inner ground of the writer—a very unfamiliar land?

The intensity of this inward beam can strain both the eye and the mind.

It may well ask too much.

Perhaps the meeting of the writer and what he writes is best left as separate entities.

IS IT JUST ME?

I'd really like to know: Is what I stick on these 3x5 cards just me, or are they thoughts that run within all of us either consciously or unconsciously?

Doesn't anyone else besides me sometimes need to see, in print, stuff that runs within?

I am secure, yet insecure. Wouldn't it be nice to know I'm not alone in this?

And darn it, I wish somebody else would write their thoughts down to help let me know it's O.K.

—"Me too!"

Made in the USA
Lexington, KY
14 April 2015